# La Malinche

## The Princess Who Helped
## Cortés Conquer the Aztec Empire

By Francisco Serrano

Illustrated by Pablo Serrano

Translated by Susan Ouriou

Groundwood Books
House of Anansi Press
Toronto  Berkeley

# Horses and Women

Early in the spring of 1519, a fleet of eleven large Spanish warships arrived at the mouth of the Tabasco River on the southern shore of what is now called the Gulf of Mexico. They were transporting more than five hundred soldiers under the command of the intrepid Captain Hernán Cortés. The ships had set sail from the island of Cuba a month and a half earlier to explore the lands of Mexico. The Spaniards prepared to go ashore to replenish their supplies of water and food.

Hidden among the coastal mangrove trees, an army of thousands of indigenous warriors lay in ambush, carrying spears, machetes and arrows. The minute the Spaniards set foot on land, the indigenous chiefs ordered them to leave or face a fierce battle. Through a Spaniard who had been captured by the Maya of that region several years earlier and had learned to speak their language, Cortés tried to convince the chiefs that his intent was not to wage war. He asked that they let the expedition continue. But the warriors refused and proceeded to beat their drums and sound their conch shells, threatening to kill the intruders.

Cortés believed that the only avenue left was confrontation and, in mid-April, after several skirmishes, he managed to defeat the warriors not far from the town of Centla. During that battle, the Spaniards brought out their horses for the first time. The animals made a marked impression on their enemies, who had never seen anything like them before and took them for monsters.

The defeated Tabascans agreed to declare peace, and the chiefs presented Cortés with many gifts — gold, jewelry, food and twenty indigenous women slaves to make their "bread," or maize tortillas. One girl stood out from the other women. She was no more than fifteen or sixteen, beautiful, intelligent and self-assured. Her name was Malinali, or Malitzin. The Spaniards baptized the women, and Malinali was given the name Marina.

# The Advantage of Speaking Three Languages

Cortés and his soldiers continued their advance. A few days later, in a place now known as San Juan de Ulúa, the great Moctezuma's emissaries came to greet them. Moctezuma, the Aztec emperor of Mexico-Tenochtitlan, was aware that the Spaniards had landed on territory under his rule. He had sent his ambassadors to discover their intentions and offer gifts in an attempt to encourage them to leave. When Moctezuma's emissaries began to speak, Cortés realized that the Spaniard who spoke Maya and had been serving as his interpreter did not understand these men who spoke Nahuatl, the Aztec language. However, Malinali, or Marina, as the young slave was now known, was able to speak the emissaries' language. She could also speak Maya with the Spanish interpreter since she knew both Maya and Nahuatl.

Cortés called for Marina and the interpreter, whose name was Jerónimo de Aguilar, and through them he was able to communicate with the Aztec ambassadors. The words spoken by the ambassadors were translated by Marina into Maya and then by Aguilar into Spanish, so that Cortés could understand. Likewise, whatever Cortés said was translated by Aguilar into Maya and by Marina into Nahuatl. And so communications began.

The two groups exchanged greetings and presents. Cortés spoke of his king, the powerful ruler Charles V, and invited Moctezuma's representatives to become his king's subjects. The emissaries offered gifts to the expedition — an abundance of food, garments, feathers and several pieces of gold jewelry — awakening the Spaniards' greed. Then they insisted that the Spaniards leave.

Through his translators, Marina and Aguilar, Cortés let Moctezuma's emissaries know that he had come on behalf of a great emperor, "lord of the greater part of the world." And to impress on them his power, he ordered the Spanish soldiers to gallop by on horseback firing their weapons. This terrified the indigenous observers, who wasted no time advising Moctezuma of what they had seen and heard.

In short order, the intelligent Marina learned enough Spanish to be able to manage without Aguilar. She began to interpret directly for Cortés. Through her, the Spanish captain was able to communicate with the indigenous world. And so Marina became the bridge between two civilizations as well as the spokesperson — the tongue, or *la lengua*, as the Spaniards called her — for the invading army's leader.

*Doña Marina proved herself an excellent woman and good interpreter. This was a basic factor in our conquest.*

*Bernal Díaz del Castillo*

8

# A Princess's Past

It is not known exactly when or where Marina was born. A few historians give her birthplace as Painala, not far from Coatzacoalcos, in what is now the state of Veracruz in eastern Mexico, around 1503 or 1504. Others say she was born in Uiluta, or Huilotlan, "the place of turtledoves," in the state of Jalisco in western Mexico. Still others lean toward Xaltipan, near Acayucan, also in Veracruz, a place known for the beauty and confidence of its women. What is known is the story of her life.

Malinali, as she was first known, was the daughter and heir of chieftains of the Painala, who were vassals of the Aztecs.

While she was still a child, her father died and her mother married another chief. A son was born and, since her mother and stepfather preferred a male heir, they decided to be rid of her. They spread a rumor that she had died, but in fact either sold or gave her to merchants from Xicalanco. One of their slave's daughters had just died, and so Malinali's mother made it known that that body belonged to her daughter. The Xicalanco merchants took Malinali to Tabasco, where she lived as a slave until she was given to Cortés.

Clear-sighted, determined and courageous, Malinali-Marina soon earned Cortés' trust and respect, and eventually she became indispensable. She went everywhere with the captain, who did nothing without first consulting her. Not only was her knowledge of the indigenous language, culture and outlook invaluable to him, her sound judgment and fortitude helped to encourage and guide him. She explained to Cortés the indigenous peoples' beliefs and opinions, and relayed to them his words of warning and other communications. She was Cortés' voice in Nahuatl, the person who made it possible to inform the mighty Moctezuma of his motives and intentions in Mexico.

Over time, Marina fell in love with the daring Cortés, whom she saw to some extent as a liberator, freeing the peoples of the region from the Aztec yoke.

> The Mexica [Aztecs] admired Doña Marina and attributed her knowledge of the Spanish language to a supernatural power — her knowledge of the language had to have come to her through the gods since there was no other possible explanation.
>
> *Friar Juan de Torquemada*

# Love and Cunning

ernán Cortés was thirty-four when he arrived in Mexico. Those who knew him said he was "of good stature," with light beard and hair, "very strong, spirited and skilled in weapons." He was bold, sociable and well spoken. It is no wonder that Malinali-Marina was fascinated by the energetic, daring, intelligent man who had crossed the ocean to free her people from the tyranny of the Aztecs. Cortés, for his part, took advantage of her devotion. Through Marina, he learned that the indigenous peoples believed that he was Quetzalcóatl, the god of the wind, returning from the east to reclaim his land as had been prophesized. He used that knowledge to his advantage with Moctezuma. The Aztec emperor was fearful and tried to dissuade Cortés from making the journey to Tenochtitlan. He sent him increasingly valuable gifts, which only fanned the flames of the Spaniards' greed.

Calling on the skill of his clever interpreter who, in the words of a chronicler of the time, allowed him "to better carry out his designs and plans," a cunning Cortés began to gather intelligence on the political and military situation in the area. Then he worked to establish alliances with the chiefs in the regions he traveled through. Many of them were enemies of the Aztecs and were subject to, and deeply resentful of, their power.

Cortés used Marina to spread the word about Christianity to the people he encountered. She helped him to convince them to abandon the worship of their idols and the horrific practice of human sacrifice. He ordered the destruction of the temples in which the indigenous peoples worshipped their gods and, in their place, he erected altars and shrines on which the Spaniards placed crosses and images of the Virgin Mary.

12

13

# A Determined Captain

Although Cortés was unaware of the size and extent of the territory he had entered, he set his sights on conquering it. To ensure that his soldiers could not return to Cuba, as some hoped to do, he scuttled his ships along the coast. Then, overcoming myriad obstacles, he set out on the journey to the legendary Aztec capital. Advised by his Totonac allies, he headed for Tlaxcala, crossing the great mountain range dividing the coast from the high central valleys. Towns along the way, following orders handed down by a worried Moctezuma, gave Cortés' army a peaceful reception.

When the Tlaxcalans, old enemies of the Aztecs, heard of the Spaniards' approach, they decided to launch an attack and dispatched a large army to meet them. After many battles, the crafty Tlaxcalans made repeated offers of peace that they then ignored, promising friendship and waging war. But they were eventually defeated and agreed to work with the conquistadors. Marina played a key role in the negotiations. Her unfailing courage, wisdom and presence of mind accounted in large part for the success of the alliance between Cortés and the Tlaxcalans. The pact turned out to be a decisive one for the Conquest of Mexico.

14

> I saw how, through Doña Marina and her knowledge of the language of the land, where there was no other language at the time, the Indians came in peace and brought food to the Spaniards; and I saw how Doña Marina spoke to the Indians, both those bent on war and those who came in peace, to convince them to accept what the Marquis desired.
>
> Gonzalo Rodriguez de Ocaña

# An Ambush Uncovered

espite warnings from his new allies, the Tlaxcalans, Cortés decided to accept an invitation from Moctezuma's emissaries to proceed to the city of Cholula, knowing it would bring him even closer to Tenochtitlan. The Tlaxcalans sent a mighty army to accompany him, but since they were enemies of the Cholulans, they camped on the outskirts of the city. Meanwhile, Cholula's leaders and priests welcomed Cortés warmly. Yet in secret they mounted an ambush to rid themselves of the invaders.

An elderly woman from Cholula had taken a liking to "young, beautiful and wealthy" Marina, thinking she would make a good match for her son. And so she approached Marina, urging that she come away with her to save her life, since the Spaniards and all those accompanying them were to be killed.

Marina thanked the woman for her offer, which she pretended to accept. She verified the details of the planned ambush, asked for a bit of time to gather together her belongings and went immediately to warn Cortés of the plot being hatched against him.

Cortés was able to confirm the intelligence by interrogating several Cholulans he had taken prisoner. He decided to strike first. In his own words, "I determined to surprise rather than be surprised." He ordered the arrest and execution of several of Cholula's leaders. Then, with the help of his Tlaxcalan and Totonac allies, he attacked the city, killing thousands of men, women and children and setting fire to their homes and temples. News of the horrific massacre struck fear in the hearts of the peoples of ancient Mexico.

# Moctezuma's Magnificent Kingdom

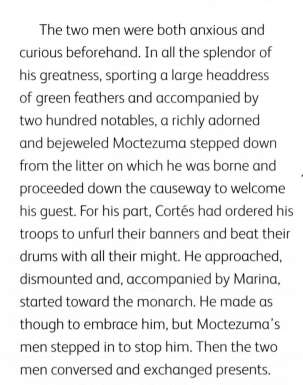

purred on by the success of his brutal actions, Cortés turned his steps toward Moctezuma's magnificent city. Early in November 1519, he marched over a pass between the two huge volcanoes looming to the east of the Valley of Mexico, Popocatépetl and Iztaccíhuatl. Ever since, the pass has been known as Paso de Cortés. From there, he and his troops could contemplate in wonder the splendor of what was, at the time, the most populated city in the world. The city's many magnificent low white buildings were built on a small island in the midst of a great aquamarine lake.

A welcoming committee of more than one thousand indigenous people greeted the Spanish soldiers and their allies. Soon afterwards the first encounter took place between the powerful Aztec emperor and the Spanish captain.

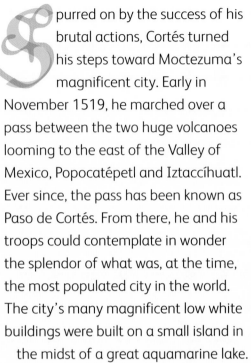

The two men were both anxious and curious beforehand. In all the splendor of his greatness, sporting a large headdress of green feathers and accompanied by two hundred notables, a richly adorned and bejeweled Moctezuma stepped down from the litter on which he was borne and proceeded down the causeway to welcome his guest. For his part, Cortés had ordered his troops to unfurl their banners and beat their drums with all their might. He approached, dismounted and, accompanied by Marina, started toward the monarch. He made as though to embrace him, but Moctezuma's men stepped in to stop him. Then the two men conversed and exchanged presents.

"Is it true that you are Moctezuma?" Cortés asked.

"Yes, I am he," replied the emperor.

The meeting between Moctezuma and Cortés is one of the most extraordinary and emotionally charged moments in history. Two civilizations, two radically different world views were face to face for the first time. And the beautiful and wise Marina was the bridge, the connecting link that allowed the two worlds to communicate. Through her understanding of the words spoken by each of the participants and her ability to interpret from one language to the other, two very different universes began to learn about each other's existence. It was the beginning of a conversation that was to end tragically.

19

# The End of an Empire

Moctezuma ordered that the visitors be housed in one of his palaces. During successive meetings with Cortés, he recounted the Aztecs' history and repeated their belief that Cortés was the returned god Quetzalcóatl. In turn, the Spanish captain stressed that he was the envoy of the powerful Charles V, and that he had come to make them his king's subjects.

A few days later, on the pretext that several Spaniards had been killed during an indigenous uprising in Veracruz, Cortés had Moctezuma seized. Then, with Marina's assistance, as always, he interrogated him about the kingdom's major features and assets — the whereabouts of its wealth, its gold mines, its most useful ports and other important information.

The Spaniards were then able to loot the Aztecs' treasures at will. They stayed on in Tenochtitlan for seven months. And when all signs pointed to the fall of the Aztec Empire without any further violence, a series of dramatic episodes resulted in an Aztec revolt, Moctezuma's death and, following a number of other incidents and atrocities, the total destruction of the city.

22

Based on what his messengers relayed to the Aztec king, Moctezuma was both in awe and fearful to see Marina, *la lengua*, giving voice to the Spaniards' words.

Fernando Alvarado Tezozomoc

# La Malinche

We will not describe the details of the Conquest of Mexico here. Like all wars, it was a terrible event that involved attacks, ambushes, retreats, treachery, accusations, persecution, hand-to-hand combat, horrific massacres, incredible acts of bravery and audacity, starvation, death and destruction. We will simply say that throughout the fifteen-month-plus campaign, Marina was always at Cortés' side. For that very reason, the Aztecs both admired and feared her. They believed that such a devoted, influential woman had to be a goddess, relaying as she did the invading chieftain's thoughts and orders. They began to call Cortés "Malinche," or "Malitzin" in Nahuatl, meaning "Marina's captain" (from "Malina," the indigenous pronunciation of Marina, and "tzin," the sign of respect). La Malinche has become the name by which Doña Marina is known today.

It is worth noting that any pictures of Marina in the original illustrated codices always show her at Cortés' side, both of them pointing their right index finger, as though clearly indicating that they are in command. The author Bernal Díaz del Castillo, who wrote the monumental book *The Discovery and Conquest of Mexico*, pointed out that "Doña Marina was a person of the greatest importance and was obeyed without question by the Indians throughout New Spain." Although Cortés rarely mentioned her in his famous *5 Letters of Cortés to the Emperor*, another conquistador, Gonzalo Rodríguez de Ocaña, stated that he occasionally heard his captain general say, "After God, we owe this conquest to Doña Marina."

Marina was Hernán Cortés' most faithful companion, interpreter and collaborator. She accompanied him when the Spanish troops fled in defeat during what became known as the Night of Sorrow, or Noche Triste, in which they lost two-thirds of their men and more than a thousand allies. And she was with him several months later, after the bloody assault on the city under siege, during which they captured the last Aztec emperor, Cuauhtémoc, as he attempted to escape by canoe on the evening of August 13, 1521.

Through Marina, the vanquished monarch said to Cortés, "Oh, captain! I have done everything in my power to defend my kingdom. Fate has not looked kindly on me. Take that dagger and kill me."

With the capture of Cuauhtémoc, the war was over and the incredible had happened. The great Tenochtitlan, one of the wonders of the world, had fallen. It was the end of the ancient indigenous civilization.

# The First Mexican

In late 1522, with the conquest over, Doña Marina gave birth to Cortés' son. They named him Martín after the conquistador's grandfather. Martín Cortés was the first *mestizo*, the first-known son of a Spaniard and an indigenous woman. In other words, he was the first Mexican, and with him a new nation was born. Cortés saw to the boy's education and had him legally recognized as his son several years later, naming him his successor.

❧ The pair formed a duet, which combined eloquence with subtlety, piety with menace, sophistication with cruelty. Her loyalty to Cortés seems to have been absolute. Her value was certainly equivalent to ten bronze cannons.

*Hugh Thomas*

# Gratitude and Forgiveness

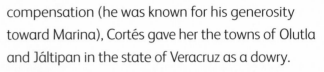

In the summer of 1524, Cortés received news that Captain Cristóbal de Olid, whom he had dispatched to explore lands to the south, had rebelled in Hibueras, today known as Honduras. Ignoring all advice to exercise caution, Cortés set out from Tenochtitlan at the head of an army to punish the rebel. He forced many of his former comrades-in-arms to accompany him and also brought along Doña Marina, the dethroned Cuauhtémoc and other captive indigenous leaders. On October 12, the large party left for Coatzacoalcos.

Near Orizaba, for reasons nobody knows, the conquistador decided to marry Doña Marina to his lieutenant, Juan Jaramillo. Marina obeyed without a murmur. "She knew how to reconcile herself to what would be," remarked one historian. Perhaps in compensation (he was known for his generosity toward Marina), Cortés gave her the towns of Olutla and Jáltipan in the state of Veracruz as a dowry.

When the army reached Coatzacoalcos, Cortés ordered a group of local indigenous chieftains to be brought to him. Among them were Marina's mother, who had sold her to merchants when she was still a girl, and her half-brother. They were both afraid when they saw her, thinking she would seek revenge. However, Marina calmed their fears and told them that they were forgiven — that when they sold her they did not know what they were doing. She gave them gifts of jewelry and clothing and said that she was "fortunate to be Christian and to have a son by her lord and master Cortés." And then she asked them to return to their town.

27

# The Beginning of the End

After several days in Coatzacoalcos, Cortés continued his march southeast. In the province of Acalan, he received news that the captive Cuauhtémoc was planning to kill him. Without verifying the information, he called on Marina's services to interrogate Cuauhtémoc. The captive denied that it was true but nonetheless stated, "Malitzin, for some time now I have known you would have to kill me. God asks it of you…"

Without further ado, Cortés — some say persuaded by Marina — cruelly and unjustly ordered that Cuauhtémoc and the other rulers be hanged from a tree and that their bodies be decapitated.

The expedition to Hibueras was the beginning of the end for Cortés. Some historians think that his misfortunes began when he separated from Marina. Be that as it may, the advance deep into the region's marshes, rivers and jungles proved to be disastrous. After months of arduous marches, during which they lost many men and horses, the Spaniards and their indigenous companions were starving, disoriented and exhausted. They finally managed to reach Hibueras only to learn that Cristóbal de Olid had died. The long trek turned out to have been in vain.

The battered expedition returned to Tenochtitlan in mid-June 1526, one year and eight months after their departure. On the return voyage, Marina gave birth to Juan Jaramillo's daughter, who was given the name María. The couple settled down in a house on Calle de Medinas (now known as Calle de Cuba), a street in the heart of the city of Mexico, where they were respected and prosperous.

Little is known of Marina's last days. It is thought that she died during a smallpox epidemic in 1527, even before she reached the age of twenty-five. She was likely buried in the church of the Holy Trinity, later converted into the Santa Clara monastery, which no longer exists.

# Myth and Reality

Malinali-Marina, or La Malinche, is a controversial figure who continues to give rise to discussion and debate. For some, she is the symbolic mother of all Mexicans. Others see her as a traitor who betrayed her people by aiding and favoring the conquistadors. There is even a term in Mexico — *malinchismo* — that refers to a Mexican who prefers foreign values, customs or traditions to his or her own. Some observers believe that she was a remarkable woman who forged the Mexican nationality and who had few options when confronted with the disruptive appearance of the Spanish soldiers and their mighty captain. They not only freed her from slavery but also gave her the means of acquiring prestige and authority.

The memory of the princess who helped conquer an empire is alive and well in many ways. A volcano in the state of Tlaxcala and several peaks and hills throughout Mexico bear the name Malinche. The Danza de la Malinche is part of many regional religious celebrations. And there is even still a superstition about a ghost often identified with La Malinche — a woman dressed in white with whom any encounter is fatal. She appears to travelers on moonlit nights along riverbanks or the shores of lagoons lamenting the death of her children. The specter, also called La Llorona, is known from a legend dating back to pre-Hispanic times. It is said she was the goddess Cihuacóatl, who roamed the streets of Tenochtitlan at night shortly before the arrival of the Spaniards foretelling the destruction of the Aztecs. She continues to instill fear in the townspeople of Mexico.

It is important to re-examine the myth and study this unique character from history. Only then can we understand her true significance.

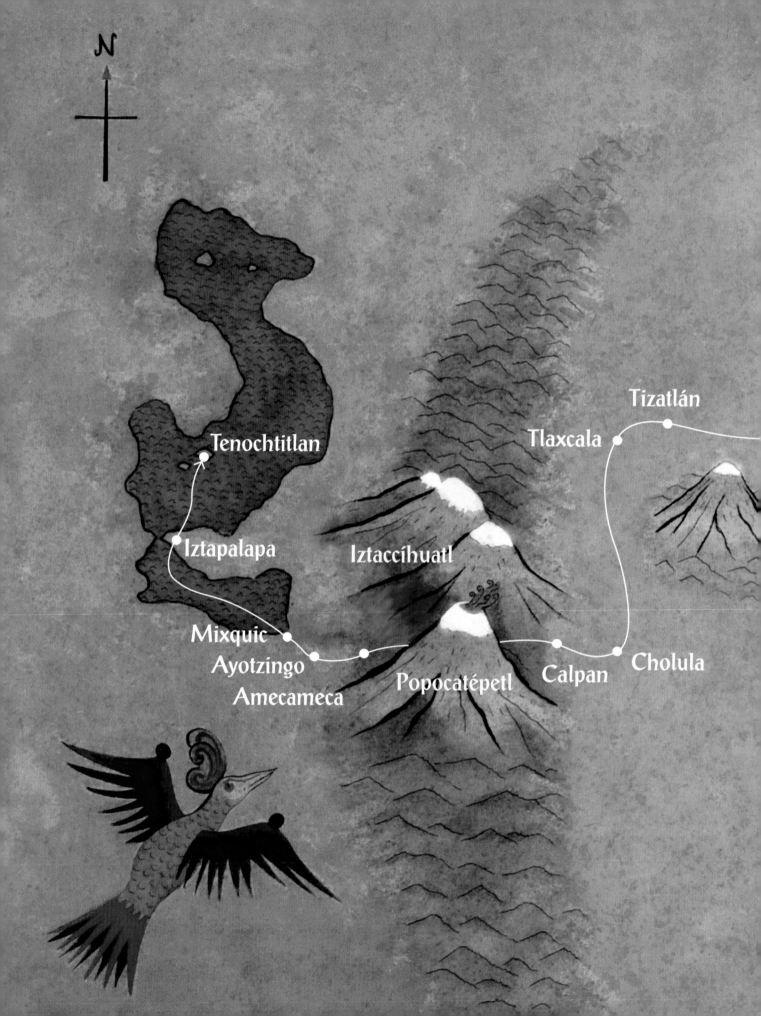

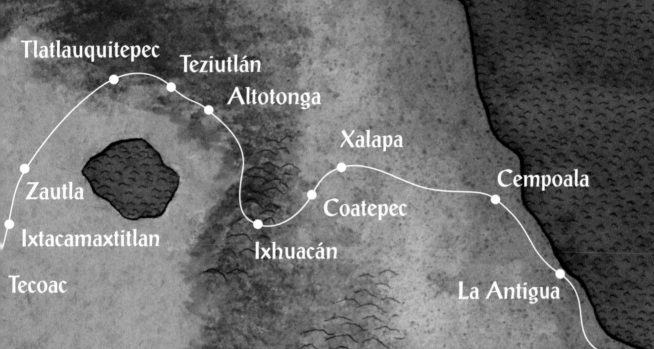

Gulf of Mexico

Tlatlauquitepec

Teziutlán

Altotonga

Zautla

Xalapa

Ixtacamaxtitlan

Cempoala

Coatepec

Tecoac

Ixhuacán

La Antigua

San Juan de Ulúa

In 1519, Hernán Cortés and his army sailed from Cuba to the southern shore of what is now known as the Gulf of Mexico. There he met Malinali, or La Malinche, the young indigenous princess who became his interpreter, and the Spanish began the march toward the Aztec city of Tenochtitlan. This map shows the towns they passed through, conquering indigenous peoples along the way. In 1521, Tenochtitlan fell to the Spaniards, and Cortés built Mexico City on its ruins.

# Epilogue

Although Hernán Cortés was greeted as a hero on his return from the Hibueras expedition in June 1526, he discovered that during his absence the government of Mexico City had fallen into serious disorder. Plotted against and betrayed by his former comrades and subordinates, he was stripped of his property, dismissed from his posts as governor, captain general and administrator of the peoples of the land, and banished from the city.

In early 1528, he traveled to Spain, where he was obliged to undergo a trial. He was accused of skimming large quantities of gold from the tax meant for the king and was suspected of having murdered his first wife, Catalina Juárez. The charges were dropped, and Cortés was able to lobby the king to restore his rank of captain general and bestow on him the title of Marquis of the Valley of Oaxaca, with dominion over many peoples and vassals. But the famous conquistador never regained the right to govern the lands he had conquered. In 1530, he returned to Mexico and devoted the next ten years to exploring the Pacific Ocean coast. In 1535, he discovered Baja California and sailed the gulf separating the peninsula from the continent. Its English name is Gulf of California, but in Spanish it bears the name Mar de Cortés (Sea of Cortés) in his honor.

Cortés returned to Spain in 1540, and the following year he was part of the Algiers expedition in North Africa to fight pirates infesting the Mediterranean Sea. But the expedition turned out to be a disastrous failure for Charles V's navy.

Over the following years, Cortés tried in vain to obtain an audience with the king. In ill health, poor and scorned, he died on December 2, 1547, in Castilleja de la Cuesta, a town not far from Seville, without returning to his property in America.

Cortés was buried in Seville, but his remains were later transported to Mexico City and were reburied in the church of the Hospital of Jesus. His death marked the end of the great Spanish conquistadors of the Renaissance.

# Chronology

**1485** Birth of Hernando, Fernando or Hernán Cortés, now known as Hernán Cortés, in the city of Medellín, in the Extremadura region of Spain.

**1502** Motecuhzoma Xocoyotzin, commonly known as Moctezuma, is chosen as the ninth ruler of Mexico-Tenochtitlan.

**c. 1503** Birth of Malinali, later called Doña Marina, near Coatzacoalcos (perhaps in Painala), in the southeast of the present-day state of Veracruz, the daughter of local chieftains.

**1504** Death of Queen Isabel of Castile in Spain. Hernán Cortés, a young man of nineteen, reaches the island of Española in search of riches.

**1505** Severe famine cripples the peoples of the Valley of Mexico.

**1506** Charles V is appointed king of Spain.

**1508** The Aztecs believe they have been witness to bad omens — ghosts and a white flag, the color of clouds, floating in the sky.

**1510** Nezahualpilli, Lord of Tezcoco, is consulted by Moctezuma and prophesizes great calamities and misfortune leading to the destruction of indigenous cities and the end of the indigenous world. During that same period there is a solar eclipse, a fire in the Huitzilopochtli temple and a comet that seems to fall to earth. Moctezuma's sister describes her vision of white-bearded men bearing banners and wearing feathers on their heads.

**1511** Rumors circulate that a huge bird with a man's head was found next to Tenochtitlan's Great Temple. Jerónimo de Aguilar and Gonzalo Guerrero are shipwrecked off the coast of Yucatán.

**1512** King Ferdinand of Aragon, known as Ferdinand the Catholic, unites the kingdoms of Castile and Navarre, consolidating Spain's territory.

**1516** In Mexico, a great comet appears in the eastern sky. The inhabitants of Tenochtitlan recount that at night a woman can be heard weeping, "Oh, my children, the hour of destruction has arrived. . . Where can I lead you to save you?"

**1517** Francisco Hernández de Córdova undertakes the first expedition to the Mexican coast. He discovers Yucatán, Campeche and Champotón.

**1518** Juan de Grijalva's expedition sails along the coast of modern-day Veracruz. Moctezuma is told of the presence of strangers traveling by sea in large vessels.

**1519** Hernán Cortés disembarks on the Mexican coast. In Tabasco, he is presented with Malinali, who becomes his interpreter. The Spanish captain founds the city of Villa Rica de la Veracruz. He destroys his ships and begins the march toward Tenochtitlan. In August, Cortés and his troops set out from the city of Cempoala. In September, after various battles, they manage to defeat the Tlaxcalans. In mid-October, the Cholula massacre takes place. In early November, the Spaniards cross the pass between the two volcanoes, Popocatépetl and Iztaccíhuatl, and contemplate in wonder the magnificence of great Tenochtitlan. On November 8, the invading army enters the Aztec capital. At a site on the present-day Calle de Pino Suárez, the first encounter between Moctezuma and Cortés takes place.

**1520** Cortés abandons Mexico-Tenochtitlan to fight Pánfilo de Narváez. The Great Temple massacre takes place. The war between the Aztecs and the Spaniards begins. In late June, Moctezuma dies. In September, Cuitláhuac is chosen as Tenochtitlan's new *tlatoani*, or great speaker. Two months later, near the end of November, the new king dies of smallpox. The young Cuauhtémoc, Lord of Tlatelolco, is chosen to replace him.

**1521** On May 30, the siege of Tenochtitlan begins. On August 13, Cuauhtémoc and his retinue are taken prisoner. After a seventy-five-day siege, the great Tenochtitlan falls to the Spaniards. The construction of the new city of Mexico begins.

**1522** Martín Cortés is born, son of Marina and the conquistador.

**1524** Cortés travels to Hibueras. Near Orizaba, he decides to marry Marina to one of his lieutenants, Juan Jaramillo. Pedro de Alvarado founds the city of Guatemala.

**1525** Using the pretext of a planned rebellion to justify his actions, Cortés sends Cuauhtémoc to his death.

**c. 1527** Doña Marina, known as La Malinche, dies during a smallpox epidemic and is buried in the church of the Holy Trinity, later converted into the Santa Clara monastery, which no longer exists.

**1547** Hernán Cortés dies in poverty and ill health in Spain. His remains are eventually buried in the church of the Hospital of Jesus in Mexico City.

# Glossary

**Cihuacóatl** Aztec goddess of motherhood and fertility.

**codices** Plural form of codex, a book in manuscript form.

**conquistador** Spanish conqueror, especially of the Americas in the 1500s.

**decapitate** To cut off the head.

**Doña** Lady or madam.

**dowry** Money or property that a woman brings to her husband upon marriage.

**emissary** Messenger sent on a mission.

**indigenous** Originating in a place; native.

*la lengua* The tongue.

*malinchismo* Person who prefers foreign values, customs or traditions to his or her own.

**marquis** Nobleman from Europe, above a count and below a duke.

*mestizo* Person of mixed blood, especially of indigenous Latin American and European ancestry.

**Nahuatl** Language spoken by the Aztecs and other indigenous peoples of Mexico and Central America.

**pre-Hispanic** Time before the Spanish Conquest of the Americas.

**Quetzalcóatl** Aztec god of the wind.

**retinue** Followers or attendants.

**scuttle** To sink a ship by making holes in the bottom.

*tlatoani* Great speaker or ruler.

**vassal** Person given land and protection in return for paying honor and service to another; servant.

# Sources

Many works were consulted in the creation of this book, including the following period sources:

Alva Ixtlixóchitl, Fernando de, *Obras históricas*, Edición de Alfredo Chavero. Mexico City: Editora Nacional, 1965.

Chimalpain Cuauhtlehuantzin, Domingo Francisco de San Antón Muñón, *Relaciones originales de Chalco Amaquemecan*, Paleografía, traducción y glosa de Silvia Rendón. Mexico City: Fondo de Cultura Económica, 1982.

Códice Florentino, Edición facsimilar, Gobierno de la Republica Mexicana. Vol. 3. Florence: Editorial Giunti Barbera, 1979.

Cortés, Hernán, *Cartas de Relación*. Mexico City: Editorial Porrúa, 1960.

Díaz del Castillo, Bernal, *Historia verdadera de la conquista de la Nueva España*, Edición, índices y prólogo de Carmelo Sáenz de Santa María. Mexico City: Editorial Patria, 1983.

Durán, Fray Diego, *Historia de las Indias de Nueva España e islas de la tierra firme*, Edición de Ángel María Garibay. Mexico City: Editorial Porrúa, 1967.

El lienzo de Tlaxcala, Edición de Mario de la Torre. Mexico City: Cartón y papel de México, 1983.

Sahagún, Fray Bernardino de, *Historia general de las cosas de Nueva España*, Edición de Ángel María Garibay. Vol. 4. Mexico City: Editorial Porrúa, 1956.

Torquemada, Fray Juan de, *Monarquía indiana*, Introducción por Miguel León Portilla. Vol. 1. Mexico City: Editorial Porrúa, 1986.

Page 8: "lord of…world." Hernán Cortés, trans. by J. Bayard Morris, *5 Letters of Cortés to the Emperor* (London: Dorset, 1928); "Doña Marina…conquest." Bernal Díaz del Castillo, *Historia verdadera de la conquista de la Nueva España*, Edición, índices y prólogo de Carmelo Sáenz de Santa María (Mexico City: Editorial Patria, 1983); 10: "The Mexica…possible explanation." Fray Juan de Torquemada, *Monarquía indiana*, Introducción por Miguel León Portilla (Mexico City: Editorial Porrúa, 1986), vol. 1; 12: "of good stature," and "very strong…weapons." Cortés; "to better…plans," Francisco López de Gómara in José Luis Martínez, *Hernán Cortés* (Mexico City: Universidad Nacional Autónoma de México y Fondo de Cultura Económica, 1990); 14: "I saw…desired." Gonzalo Rodríguez de Ocaña in Hugh Thomas, *The Conquest of Mexico* (London: Hutchinson, 1993); 16: "young…wealthy" Díaz; "I determined…surprised." Cortés; 22: "Based on…words." Fernando Alvarado Tezozómoc, *Crónica mexicana* (1598), annot. by Manuel Orozco y Berra (Mexico City: Editorial Porrúa, 1987); 24: "Doña Marina… Spain." Bernal Díaz del Castillo, trans. by A.P. Maudslay, *The Discovery and Conquest of Mexico* (Cambridge, MA: Da Capo Press, 2003); 25: "After God…Marina." Gonzalo Rodríguez de Ocaña in Thomas; 26: "The pair…cannons." Thomas; 27: "She knew…be," Martínez; "fortunate to…Cortés." Díaz, trans. by Maudslay; 28: "Malitzin, for…you…" Ibid; 35: "Oh, my…you." Fray Bernardino de Sahagún, *Historia general de las cosas de Nueva España*, Edición de Ángel María Garibay (Mexico City: Editorial Porrúa, 1956), vol. 4.

# Further Reading

*Ancient Aztec: Archaeology Unlocks the Secrets of Mexico's Past* by
   Tim Cooke. Washington D.C.: National Geographic, 2007.
*Broken Shields* by Claudia Burr, Krystyna Libura and Maria Cristina
   Urrutia. Toronto: Groundwood Books, 1997.
*Hernán Cortés* by Heather Lehr Wagner. New York: Chelsea House,
   2009.
"La Malinche: Creator or Traitor" by R. Michael Conner. Translator
   Interpreter Hall of Fame, http://www.tihof.org/honors/malinche.
   htm.
*What the Aztecs Told Me* by Krystyna Libura, Maria Cristina Urrutia and
   Claudia Burr. Toronto: Groundwood Books, 1997.

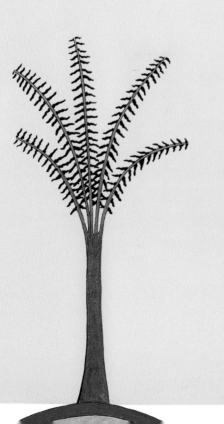

First published in Spanish as *La princesa que ayudó a conquistar
un imperio: Historia de la Malinche* by CIDCLI
Copyright © 2011 by CIDCLI, S.C.
Text copyright © 2011 by Francisco Serrano
First published in English in Canada and the USA in 2012 by
Groundwood Books
English translation copyright © 2012 by Susan Ouriou

Groundwood Books / House of Anansi Press
110 Spadina Avenue, Suite 801, Toronto, Ontario M5V 2K4
or c/o Publishers Group West
1700 Fourth Street, Berkeley, CA 94710

We acknowledge for their financial support of our publishing
program the Canada Book Fund (CBF).

Library and Archives Canada Cataloguing in Publication
Serrano, Francisco
La Malinche : the princess who helped Cortés conquer the Aztec
empire / by Francisco Serrano ; illustrated by Pablo Serrano ;
translated by Susan Ouriou.
Translation of: La princesa que ayudó a conquistar un imperio :
historia de la Malinche.
ISBN 978-1-55498-111-3
1. Marina, ca. 1505-ca. 1530 — Juvenile literature. 2. Cortés,
Hernán, 1485-1547 — Juvenile literature. 3. Mexico — History
— Conquest, 1519-1540 — Juvenile literature. 4. Aztec women —
Biography — Juvenile literature.
I. Serrano, Pablo  II. Ouriou, Susan  III. Title.
F1230.M373S4713 2012    j972'.02092    C2012-902189-X

Design by Rogelio Rangel
Printed and bound in China

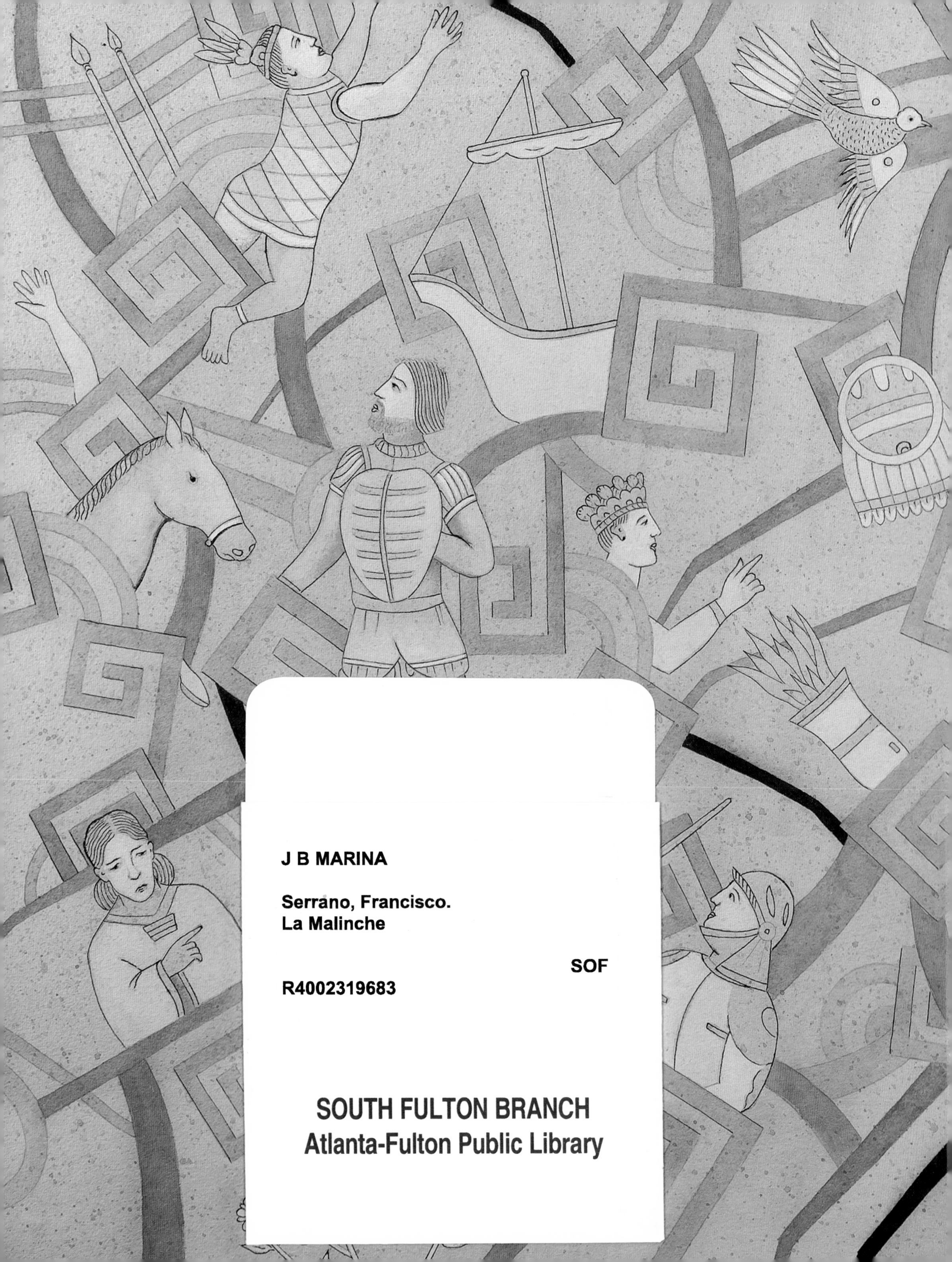